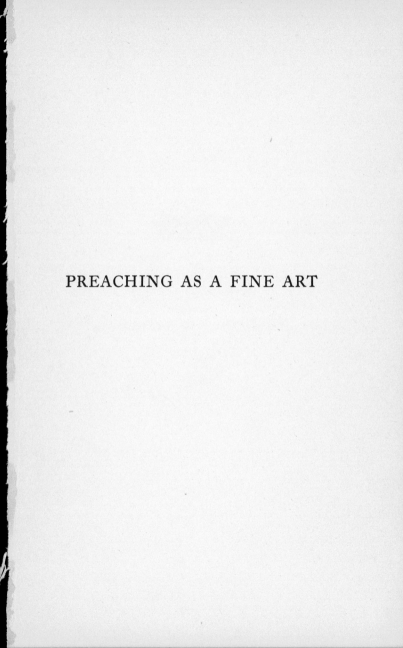

# PREACHING AS A FINE ART

THE MACMILLAN COMPANY
NEW YORK · BOSTON · CHICAGO · DALLAS
ATLANTA · SAN FRANCISCO

MACMILLAN & CO., LIMITED
LONDON · BOMBAY · CALCUTTA
MELBOURNE

THE MACMILLAN CO. OF CANADA, LTD.
TORONTO

# PREACHING AS A FINE ART

BY

ROLAND COTTON SMITH, D.D.

*Rector Emeritus, St. John's Church, Washington*

New York

THE MACMILLAN COMPANY

1922

To

## JOHN COTTON SMITH

AND

## WILLIAM OTIS SMITH

Praxiteles, the sculptor of old time, wrought a delicate image, but lifeless, the dumb counterfeit of beauty, endowing the stone with form; but this Praxiteles of to-day, creator of living beings by his magic, hath molded in my heart love. His works are better. Since he has transformed no stone but the spirit of the mind, graciously may he mold my character, that when he has formed it he may have within me a temple of love, even my soul.

MELEAGER.

v

# PREFACE

These lectures, delivered before the Faculty and Students of Divinity Schools in Alexandria, Cambridge and New York, have grown out of the conviction that it is absolutely unnecessary for any sermon ever to be dull or unconvincing.

If the fault were with the man we might lose hope, but every preacher has within him the power to move the human soul. If the trouble lay in the message, we might well despair, but the message wears the same glory yesterday, today and forever. That the fault lies in the method gives us encouragement and a renewed hope. For the method can be changed and must be changed.

My friend Gerald Stanley Lee is kind enough to think that I have pointed out the right method, and is helping me to reach a larger audience by means of his arresting and compelling voice.

ROLAND COTTON SMITH.

# CONTENTS

# INTRODUCTION

I FIND myself actuated by two feelings in this little introductory word to the spirit in these pages of Roland Cotton Smith. One is a curious, persistent, wayward feeling of eulogy, of delighting in something that has been taken from my life, something that I would recapture if I only could—that I must recapture if I only can—and hand on to the lives of others.

The other feeling is a feeling that has grown as I began to write.

The first feeling I have of Roland Cotton Smith is one of companionship with thousands of other people standing in line at the doors waiting for a chance to hear him in that quaint, honest, lovable old church in Washington opposite the White House. There comes upon me, as I picture the little church in my mind without him, a sense of vanishing, and my mind sweeps past the fact that I saw him yesterday in the street, into a deep and poignant regret that that part of Washington it was to me on a Sunday morning to stand in the porches of Saint John's and pray for him and pray with him before he lifted his voice to his people and his God, is gone. I cannot be reconciled to it—to the fact that the strangers who will read his words in this little book can now no longer go and stand as I have stood and thousands of others in the porches of Saint John's waiting and praying and worshiping with Roland Cotton Smith for sixty minutes, and then going away remembering it and worshiping with it and with the spirit of it, Sunday morning after Sunday morning, many years.

So here I am in the act (as any reader can see for himself) of strangely, perversely from sheer gladness of memory, writing of a glowing man—a man I met in the street yesterday—a man who may be pouring himself out to me to-morrow—as if he were dead!

And all because next Sunday morning in Washington, with hundreds of others in the Sunday morning sunshine in Lafayette Square, before the doors of the little church opposite that serene, unconscious-looking White House, forgetting its dreams and fears and quarrels and memories and sins behind the gracious trees, I shall not be standing waiting in line to find a place to worship God and to delight in the glory of the world, with the soul of a child and with the voice of Roland Cotton Smith!

I know, of course, that I ought not to be doing it—writing a eulogy of a man—almost an obituary of him, almost before his own face; but the sense that the artist has, the sense of wanting to recapture and to hand on to others, of being unwilling to give up and to lay something in one's life forever away, is too much for me. To a man who perpetuates himself in literature, the tragic and baffling silence of the soul of the preacher, when the mere sound of his mere voice has died away, seems almost an act of violence.

However high and pure and fine it may be, the sense that the spirit of a man, in all its rugged integrity, its heaping up and focusing of power and of delight, has become or is going to become a vague glorious mist of scattered human lives—that it shall never be gathered into itself again forever, overrides something in one's mind and in one's heart. One begins wondering if it is as necessary as it looks. What is there that could be or might be done in the way of exposing ministers to other ministers, so that the coal of fire shall be lighted directly from the coal of fire and the succession be from preacher to preacher?

This is a thought that cannot but keep coming back to one—especially to one who looks forward, as I do, to the destiny of the Church in this our present day, who is wistful for its glory, jealous for its prophets, who wants to see the doors and aisles of churches haunted every Sunday with the voices of the serene and the high and the great, so that the young men shall look up to them and flock to them, and the glory of the Lord shall be renewed before the youth and His face shine upon our altars!

So anyone can see how it is. This mounting up of desire and memory and perhaps a little fear, starts one writing an introduction like this in a very unreconciled and partly unreasonable state of mind about the spoken word and about the lives and powers of the men who, like Roland Cotton Smith, give themselves whole-souled to the profession of professions.

So perhaps my reader will forgive me if—though

I meet him glowing in the street in the morning, though I find him exercising to the full before my eyes his right to live—I am allowed to lose my sense of humor, draw close to what might seem a kind of glossed-over obituary, for the first minute or so in writing of a man who has been to me for years a national necessity in thinking of Washington, the thought of whom had become a little happy island for my soul in the National Capital, upon whose mind I had come to look—right across from the President so—as a kind of spiritual wing on the White House!

.        .        .        .        .        .        .

So not unnaturally when I was sitting the other day under a tree in Gramercy Park with a big envelope in my hand and took out an M.S. fresh from the publishers and came on the glowing and gracious words of this little book, there came to the surface as I read, a new, sudden and revealing desire. I saw what I saw. As I turned page after page I saw the little porches of the little Saint John's expand, I saw many thousands of people standing in their hearts with me in the porches of Saint John's. I saw that the voice that had become a part of the National Capital to me might now be freed, might now go forth, might now become a part of the national capital of the spirit of a nation.

It is a reassuring and fortifying fact for the churches of this land, that a valid voice like this, gracious and simple, full of a high courage, a delight in God and a happy hope for all mankind, shall now in these richer, later years, in its spirit of unquenchable childlikeness and boundless youth and the full tide of its powers, be more generally and widely heard than it could be heard before.

I did not think of this on the first page. I merely thought of the listening young men at Alexandria and wanted to be there. Then I began wanting the young men's churches—the ones they came out of —the ones they were going to preach in, to be there.

Then I took out my fountain pen and a bit of paper and sitting on the bench under the big tree with Teddy bears and nurses and children's voices all around, I began making these vestibule remarks to the soul of Roland Cotton Smith. I began to see that the words that were spoken to the young men at Alexandria could all be spoken to thousands of others.

I like to think that in the impulse that led him to give up the recurring demands and cares of his parish in Washington, he has but freed his spirit for being a missioner to the churches at large, that the experience I have had in going about from church to church to hear him in New York is one people are going to have everywhere. As an evangel—an evangel relighting and rededicating the altars of a great and weary and troubled church there goes forth the spirit of Roland Cotton Smith.

I see him continuing the vision of this little book —going from pulpit to pulpit interpreting a great profession—interpreting in each preacher's pulpit each preacher to his own people and interpreting the people to their preachers.

Of course the essential idea in what is said about

preaching in these pages is one that Roland Cotton Smith, like all true preachers, is more successful in dramatizing than he is in expressing. I cannot disentangle from the sound of a voice and the presence of a personality, just what these written words will bring to others, but it has come to me as a most refreshing and quickening experience—this interpretation of a great profession, at once so eloquent and yet so dumb, so pointing beyond itself, so full of the simple speechlessness and hope of the New Testament and of little children, so high and so clear and withal, with a kind of stern beauty in it like the mingling of a boy-choir and of the voice of God!

It is indeed good to the heart to have called up before one in the nick of time, in this great, swift, tragic moment of our world, this all-believing, all-claiming conception—this almost redeeming conception, half tradition, and half prayer, of what preaching is really like.

GERALD STANLEY LEE.

# PREACHING AS A FINE ART

# Preaching as a Fine Art

# Preaching as a Fine Art

## I

### THE PREACHER AS ARTIST

THE President and Faculty of this school at Alexandria have honored me by their invitation to speak to you. One so honored cannot help going back in thought to the ancient Alexandrian school and its rich contribution to literature and the arts. And I am moved by what is more than a mere coincidence of names to speak to you on "Preaching as a Fine Art." Do not think that I am trying to bring coals to Newcastle, or ideas to Alexandria, the mother of great preachers; I have come to help to keep alive the fine traditions, and to take the coals from off the Altar that is already here, to touch your lips with fire.

Preaching as a Fine Art: I do not intend to be trapped into definitions. Definitions, as a rule, confine, rather than define. If any one can prove to me that, strictly speaking, preaching is not a fine art, I do not know and I do not care. I am using the title more as a suggestion than as an argument. If murder can be considered a fine art, certainly preaching may put in its claim to the same consideration. If it is not one of the sisters, it is a first cousin. And the preacher has much to learn from the masters of the arts.

3

Like the sculptor (for sculpture is the first of the fine arts to suggest itself), the preacher has his vision, his material, his tools and his creative power. We are to examine this process and find out what vision and material and tools and power belong to the preacher.

The image of God is the preacher's vision, the nature of man is the preacher's material, the sermon is the preacher's tool, and the Spirit of God within him, coöperating with his spirit, is the preacher's creative power. Preaching, therefore, is the creation of the nature of man into the image of God, as expressed in the person of Jesus Christ, by means of words issuing from the preacher's inner spirit. Now, I beg you to accept this statement and not challenge it in your minds and we will see, I hope, what it means later on.

If the nature of man is the material upon which the preacher artist works, we see to what point his artistry and skill are directed. It changes our conception of the sermon. The sermon is not an end, it is a means! It is not the material, it is a tool, but, like all subordinate things, important in the great scheme. And so you see that when I am speaking of preaching as a fine art, I am not thinking primarily of the sermon; of the fine art of writing or of speaking; of the art of constructing sentences, of the art which lies in literature: all that is subordinate and important, but after all it is but the fashioning and the polishing of the tool to do its perfect work. A man by his art may fashion a sermon into the finest bit of literature; he may deliver it with the tongue of men and of angels, but if that is all, it lies a beautiful tool within his impotent hand. That is not what we mean by the fine art of preaching.

And that brings us to a fundamental principle: The responsibility of a preacher rests not in the giving of a truth, but in the other man's reception of the truth. A preacher cannot say—here is the seed of the truth of the spirit and I sow it broadcast among thorns and on stony ground and now and then on good soil, and my responsibility ends there. That is just where his responsibility as an artist begins. His work and his art are with the stony ground, to do away with the stones; to rid the soil of the thorns; to create good soil.

I ask you, in this connection, to read the poem Sir Galahad, by Edgar Lee Masters, which is much too long to quote, and to read all of him if you wish to be a preacher:

> "He had studied
> The properties of soils and fertilizers
> And when he heard the field had failed to raise
> Potatoes, beans and wheat, he simply said:
> There are other things to raise; the question is
> Whether the soil is suited to the things
> He tried to raise, or whether it needs building.
> . . . The field is his, he said,
> Who can make something grow.
>     And so this field
> Of waving wheat along which we were driving
> Was just the very field the scare-crow man
> Had failed to master."

The preacher who delivers a fine sermon and finds fault with the soil of the human heart for the rejection of its truth is a scare-crow man and has failed miserably in his art. "The field is his, who can make something grow."

I can, perhaps, open the subject more fully by illustrating what has already been said by showing what I myself am trying to do!—at the same time throwing its light forward on what we are going to say.

I have come here not simply to talk to you about preaching but to *make* you *preachers*. My art, if I have any, does not consist in writing and delivering two lectures, satisfied if I can put some truth into more or less good form, speaking out of an experience of two score years, leaving you to take it or pass it by, as you please. My art consists in taking the truth out of my own experience as it has been revealed to me, and putting it in such a form that it will arrest your attention, and fix itself in your memory; communicate spirit; open your eyes; unloose your tongue and make you preachers of the word of God. And so these talks are not ends in themselves to be praised or condemned for their epigrams or ornaments. They are as nothing and worse than nothing, if they cannot make something grow. If I cannot make you better preachers by what I have written, I have failed. And so in my thought of what I am to say to you, I begin with *you*. In one way I do not know any of you. I cannot tell your names, but in a deeper sense I know you well; your high ideals; your desire to make

God's ways known to men, to make this world a better place to live in. I know of your dreams in the secret places of your heart, of what you are going to be and do. Some of you are dull, some brilliant. Some of you are lazy, some industrious; but whether you are considered dull or brilliant, lazy or industrious, this one thing I know about you, and upon this one thing I build: each one of you can be a great preacher. Each one of you can be an artist to fashion the nature of a man into the likeness of Jesus Christ and the image of God. It will take everything that is in you, your blood and sinew. You will have to toil as the great artists have to toil. Nevertheless, each one of you can be a great preacher. That one thing I know and upon that I build. Each one of you has a spirit more wonderful and powerful than you ever dream of. And it can be moved by the spirit of God and you become a creator among the things of the spirit of man.

I also know many things about you. You have crude and wrong notions about preaching. You think that if you can write a good sermon, that if your thought is good, your sentences correct, and the literary form fine, and if you will also take lessons in elocution and master your delivery, you will be a good preacher. Whereas in reality, you have only fashioned your tools.

Now, all this I know about you, and I must put my talk in such a form that you will realize it. My responsibility does not end when I have told you in so many words that each one of you can be a

preacher.   I must so use my tool that it will engrave
the truth upon your mind and heart, and start eternal forces at work that will make you a preacher.
And so, if I am not skillful in fashioning my
tool, I ought to be, only polishing it when it needs
polishing, sharpening it at the point where it cuts,
leaving out everything superfluous, constructing my
tool for the one purpose of opening your eyes.

But the process is far more subtle than that.
Words are easily misunderstood.   They often convey an opposite meaning.   I come to you out of a
long experience.   Behind all my word there ought to
be—and if there is not, it is of no value—an un-
heard communication of my spirit with your spirit.
Just in proportion as I am untrue and false in myself
the spirit will not go out of me.   If I am insincere,
if I speak of that which I do not know, and tell of
things I have not seen, I shall fail.   On the other
hand, if I am true and not false, if I speak of the
truth which I have seen and known, of the things
which I myself have handled, my spirit will go out
of me, even ahead of my words, to interpret the
words, and it will begin in subtle and unseen ways
to mold and build upon your spirit, opening your
eyes, stirring your will, creating in you the power
to preach.   And I also come here with this tremen-
dous conviction, that while thousands can do it
better, no one else in the whole wide world can do
it just as I can do it.   God has given me a certain
experience.   I see truth at my particular angle.   My
vision is unlike anyone else's vision, vouchsafed to
me alone.   This is my opportunity.   I may die to-

night and never speak again.   While it is day I may
have something given me by God that may make you
a preacher.   Therefore, this is not a quiet lecture
to pass away the time; it can be an eternal moment
fraught with vast possibilities.   Here in God's
workroom one man is struggling to take the truth as
he sees it and build it into the nature of another man.
It is possible that out of the struggle some great
preacher may be born.   That spirit of adventure,
with the possibility that at any moment the divine
hand will guide the human touch and create a masterpiece, is the life and the joy of the artist.

I have used what I am trying to do as an illustration of what a preacher ought to do; to throw
light, in a general way, upon our further study of
preaching as a fine art.

Of course you may say to me: "You are speaking
exactly as if some man was sitting for his portrait,
or as if there was some one soul constantly in your
studio upon which you might work and create.
Whereas the preacher has to do with natures that
come and go, and his work must of necessity be hap-
hazard and general."   That is so.   And here we
strike at the root of the matter.   This is what
makes preaching the most difficult art in the world.
I ask you to read, in this connection, Matthew
Arnold's "Epilogue to Lessing's Laocoön."

"One noon as through Hyde Park we walked
My friend and I, by chance we talked
Of Lessing's famed Laocoön
And after we a while had gone

On Lessing's track, and tried to see
What painting is, what poetry
Diverging to another thought,
'Ah,' cries my friend, 'but who has taught
Why music and the other arts
Oftener perform aright their parts
Than poetry?   Why she, than they
Fewer fine successes can display?
Profound yet touching, sweet yet strong,
Hath used Gœthe's, Wordsworth's song.
They yield us not, to soothe our pains
Such multitude of heavenly strains
As from the Kings of sound are blown
Mozart, Beethoven, Mendelssohn.'

"While thus my friend discoursed, we pass
Out of the path and take the grass.
The grass had still the green of May
And still the emblackened elms were gay
'Behold,' I said, 'the painter's sphere!
The limits of his art appear
These, or much greater things, but caught
Like these, and in one aspect brought
In outward semblance he must give
A moment's life of things that live.'

"Still we walked on, in thoughtful mood
And now, upon the bridge we stood
Full of sweet breathings was the air,
Sound as of wandering breeze—but sound
In laws by human artists bound.
'The world of music,' I exclaimed:—
                'What a sphere
Large and profound, hath genius here.
Some source of feeling he must choose

And its locked fount of beauty use.
And through the stream of music tell
Its else unutterable spell.
To choose it rightly is his part,
And press into its inmost heart.'

"Onward we moved, and reached the Ride
Where gaily flows the human tide.
Men, with their strain of life, were here
The young, the happy, and the fair
The old, the sad, the worn, were there;
Nods, smiles and greetings and farewell
And now and then, perhaps there swells
A sigh, a tear, but in the throng
All changes fast, and hies along,
Hies, ah from whence, what native ground?
And to what goal, what ending bound?
'Behold, at last, the poet's sphere!
But who,' I said, 'suffices here?'
'For, ah, so much he has to do;
Be painter and musician too!
But clear as words can make revealing
And deep as words can follow feeling
But ah! then comes his sorest spell
Of toil—he must life's movement tell!'

"The thread which binds it all in one,
And not its separate parts alone.
Its pain and pleasure, rest and strife
His eye must travel down at full,
The long, unpausing spectacle
With faithful and relaxing force
Attend it from its primal source
From change to change and year to year
Attend it of its mid career,

Attend it to the last repose
And solemn silence of its close.

"Only a few the life-stream's shore
With safe unwandering feet explore,
They speak! the happiness divine
They feel, runs o'er in every line.
Its spell is round them like a shower
It gives them pathos, gives them power.
Beethoven, Raphael, cannot reach
The charm which Homer, Shakespeare teach
To these, to these, their thankful race
Give, then, the first, the fairest place
And brightest is their glory's sheen
For greatest hath their labour been."

Now, preaching is a greater art still. It has to accomplish even more than poetry does. The preacher, like the poet, has to view the human tide, that endless procession of human beings, passing "Ever, ever, like a river," he must life's movement know. But in addition to that, the preacher not only has, like the poet, to tell of life's movement— he must by his art *impress* life's movement. He does not draw from life and reproduce it in words. He uses words to produce life.

Matthew Arnold might have added another verse to his "Epilogue to Lessing's Laocoön," and sung in his matchless way how the preacher molds the individual nature into the divine image, and by so doing diverts life's movement from a false direction and directs life's movement into the right way. And at the end he would have had to give the preachers "the first the fairest place," but he could not have named them as he names the poets, because while the poets translate life into a book and their works follow them, preachers translate a book into life, and no one ever sees the image they have made. All that we possess of the so-called Great Preachers is their tools. Good tools, no doubt, but we can never know how they used them, nor look upon their creation in the human heart, and so we shall never know the really great ones.

I have dwelt upon this poem, and I wish that you would read it over and over again, because it starts where every preacher must start, at "Life's movement," the great stream of humanity, the crowd. For a preacher is not one on Sunday when he delivers a sermon, or on Friday and Saturday when he prepares it, and something else the other days of the week: an administrator, a pastor; he is a preacher all the days and every day, morning, noon and night. He is a preacher all the time or none of the time. Everything he sees, every book he reads, every thought, every action is a preparation and a part of his preaching. As an artist you ought not to think first of your tool. You must know what you are going to do. You must first see the divine image in the human heart and know the nature of the stubborn material that hides it. And so, before you go into your study to prepare a sermon, you ought, to become a preacher, to go into your own Hyde Park! You ought actually to come up against blind, brutal, bigoted, glorious humanity—and have the crowd, not something of a

crowd but a crowd, jostle you and perhaps hurt you.
You ought to be aware of some actual social injustice, social wrongs, and social abominations that will
arouse in you a thorough and righteous indignation.
The first thing for a preacher to do is to get mad.
I am not saying that every minister who leaves his
closet and mingles with the crowd is a preacher; he
must be a preacher and an artist before he goes
into the crowd, with a definite idea of what he is
going to do; namely, to bring out the image in this
stubborn material, just as the sculptor has to feel
the resistance of the unyielding rock. Masefield,
in his poem, "The Dauber," makes the artist ship
as a seaman and undergo indignities, and battle
with the storm in order to catch the different shades
of color in the wave. Every one who ships as a
seaman will not find the color in the storm. He
who does must be an artist before he starts his
voyage. In this connection I ask you to read Masefield's poem of "The Dauber," in order to catch the
spirit that every preacher ought to have when he
begins to wrestle with his task.

If a preacher will face humanity in the spirit of
an artist, he will realize that this great mass can be
separated into individual blocks, that humanity is
made up of individuals; that you enter humanity
through the individual; that any one person has
within himself the qualities of the mass of humanity.
And so a preacher who is preparing a sermon ought
to have some one person in mind, as the sculptor
chooses his block. I do not want to stress the figure
of the sculptor too much. It is not a perfect anal-

ogy. It is only meant to help and not to hinder. The sculptor creates his image out of that one block; the preacher may draw out the image in some person other than the one he has chosen. Nevertheless, it makes for efficiency if the preacher has one person in mind, and thinks of him as if he was actually in his work-room. If you can reach one man you can reach all men.

For here is the image of God within a man. It is blind and what you want to do is to make that image *see!* That is what all preaching is for, to make a soul see. Not first of all to make a man good; that is the means to an end, and the end is *seeing;* seeing God—seeing spiritual things. Here is a man who cannot see because of his sorrow or his sin. It does not matter what prevents the normal action. If a preacher, for instance, will prepare his sermon as if a man in sorrow was in his work-room, if he can make that man see, he will comfort that man's sorrow. And at the same time he may make some other man see and take away some other man's sin.

This is the conclusion of this particular matter:— Before you prepare your sermon, go into a crowd and be hurt by it. Know that this crowd is made up of individuals, choose some one suffering person whom you know about. Have that one person constantly in mind, as if he was in your work-shop, and work to make him see. And you will prepare a sermon that can reach all the sons of men. Keep that one thing in mind—you want that one man to see.

I have been speaking as if an artist could start work on his block of marble before he saw in his imagination the image that was within it, as if a preacher could approach an individual before he knew what was hidden within the nature of that individual. That was only for convenience. Of course a preacher must start with an overpowering conviction that every man born into this world is stamped with the divine image. More than that, the preacher as an artist must know what that divine image is, he must be able to see it in every man. He must be able to see it in every man because he has found it in himself. This is quite a different thing from reading in the Book of Genesis that God made man in His own image and accepting it as a truth to be passed on to other men. The artist preacher must have a definite realization of what the image of God is. "God is a spirit." The artist must be aware of a spirit within himself. "God is love." The artist must know in himself what love is. I am not attempting to define or describe God. I am saying that whatever the nature of God may be, the artist must find the same qualities within himself; living, loving, even as God lives and loves. Finding it in himself the artist will inevitably find it in his fellow men. It is no theory, it is not an idea: it is the actual discovery of God's character in the nature of every man. No matter how low down a man may be, no matter how encrusting and resisting may be the material, somewhere down in the dark of his nature is the image of his God. Now that conviction must become instinctive with the preacher. When he is hurt by the mob, when he is wofully disappointed in the individual, always there must be that image of God, that likeness of Christ, coming out to him from the suffocating material. And I think it a good plan for the preacher at first to say to himself when he meets any man: "Within that man is the divine image. Hail! That which is born in you is the likeness of the son of God," until it becomes an instinct to find it so.

The preacher cannot have the half-vision, seeing "men as trees walking." A man is not a tree. A man is not an animal. He may so live that the life of the tree shames him; he may fall below the life of a dog; but, unlike the tree and the dog, the man has within him the capacity for seeing. In meeting any man the artist comes to his own. Therefore the artist preacher approaches an individual not primarily because he is bad, but because fundamentally he is good. He comes to his own. Coming to it in that way the artist will discover that he does not bring faith to that nature. He finds faith there and builds upon it. Every man has faith, the entrance into and appropriation of the unseen spiritual world. As every man lives by breathing, so every man lives by faith, and cannot live a moment in this world without it. The preacher artist does not bring to a man's nature the capacity for prayer; he finds a praying man, for every man prays. Every man is in communication with the spiritual world. His spirit speaks and his spirit is answered.

Here, then, is this man in your work-room, and,

let us say, he is as spiritually blind as it is possible for a man to be. He has faith and he prays, without knowing it. And your work as an artist is to make the man's true nature assert itself and take possession of the man. Here within yourself is the power to do it. If properly connected with the supreme power, and exercised in the right way, the seeing spirit within you will in some way be communicated to him.

The artist preacher must have the seeing spirit. I am not saying merely that the preacher must be a good man, that he must practice what he preaches in order to be an example to his flock; that he must say to himself—"I must not do this and that because I will lose my influence as a preacher." What I am saying has nothing to do with that sort of thing. I am saying that the artist must practice before he can preach. Words convey a meaning, not only intellectual but spiritual. The preacher deals with spiritual values and his words must be freighted with those values. And if his words are to be freighted with spiritual values the artist must be spiritual.

It is not that you must practice what you preach, you have to preach what you practice. There is no question about it; it is a scientific proposition. The word goes from you empty unless you yourself fill it with your own spirit. It is as if a musician should say: "Here is my instrument and I want it to produce music, and I will play my fingers upon the several stops!" It will not make music until the artist breathes his own breath into the in-

strument. Here is the nature of man and I want
it to produce music and I play upon it with words.
And the music does not come and will not come
until the instrument catches the breath of the life
of the spirit that issues from my soul. You may be
a great orator, you may be a fine sermonizer, but
you cannot be a preacher unless you are a spiritual
being close to your God. And, therefore, the artist
preacher of necessity goes into his closet and shuts
his door and communes with his Father which is in
secret, so that he may be able to see the divine
image in every man and to have the power to make
the man see. This is the conclusion of this particular matter:—If you are to be an artist preacher
you must be a spiritual being very close to your God.

This is the last point in the preparation for
preaching that we shall dwell upon in this first lecture. Before we close let us go over what we have
done. If you are in a critical mood you may say
to yourself that I have not proved my thesis, that
preaching is not a fine art. I reply that I have had
no thesis. I have not tried to prove that preaching
is a fine art. You may say that I have tried to be
original and that really I have not said anything
that has not been said before. I have not tried to
be original. I have simply stated the matter as I
have found it in my own experience and I am well
aware that I have merely stated the obvious. I
have stated a number of things tentatively which
probably will not bear analysis, but they can be
brushed aside, for they have nothing to do with my
main contention. Let us, therefore, for a moment

lose sight of the artist, strip the subject and get
down to the stark, naked truth, the bare, unem-
bellished facts. You are men preparing to be
preachers. If you have had thoughts that the preparation for preaching was the preparation of the
sermon, you have been mistaken. But if you have
always looked at a sermon as a means, not an end,
you have gone a long way in your preparation, for
you have gone farther than have many so-called
preachers who are much older than you. For if
you have a clear idea that the sermon is not an end
but a means, you will have gone far in the grasping
of the fundamental principle that your responsibility does not end with the giving of truth but in the
other man's reception of it.

The whole emphasis is transferred from the sermon to the man. When you approach the man and
not the sermon you find that your work consists
not in making sentences but in making men. You
are not only translating thought and life into words
but you have also to translate words back again
into life. And that is the most difficult thing in
the world to do. When you have fastened your
attention on the nature of man, instead of on
the construction of a sermon, you are bound to come
face to face with a blind, stumbling, falling, rising humanity, ever changing, ever moving—a people that laugh and cry and bless and hurt, a world
of men full of injustice and abominations. And
you as a preacher, not as something else, not as
a reformer, a social worker, a pastor, but as a
preacher, before you can preach at all must face

it and not deny the existence of the abominations as the manner of some is. You must not go round it with an easy-going, cheerful and vapid philosophy. You as a preacher have to go through it, stunned and appalled and bruised, moved and righteously angered by it. You must then grasp the obvious truth that humanity is made up of individuals. More than that, you must practice the obvious truth that humanity is made up of individuals. If we are going to have humanity at peace, the individual has to be peaceful. That obvious truth is hardly recognized to-day. It is always supposed that a preacher sways a multitude and has little to do with the individual man. The preacher does nothing of the kind. He reaches the multitude through the individual, or he does not reach it at all. Therefore, you, if you are going to be a preacher, must reach the multitude through the individual man. You may forget all I have said about the work-shop and about imagining some man in your study and all that sort of thing. If it does not help you, throw it away. You have a perfect right to do so. But you cannot get away from the fact that you can sway the multitude only by working upon the individual man.

I have now laid the foundations for what I have further to say. Before we close, let us get back to the idea of preaching as a fine art, and think of Jesus the preacher, as the consummate artist, and so bind these two lectures together with His presence, a summing up and a prophecy, linking what

I have said to-day with what I am going to say to-morrow.

Jesus, the artist, was a preacher all the time. He preached on any day and every day of the week, for He had the one consuming passion of the artist —to create.   Here, within the nature of man was a divine image, hidden within the darkness of the material; here within Himself was the image seeing, seeing His Father God and the whole invisible world within and about the visible.   Proceeding out of that relationship was a spirit with power to touch the blinded image to make it see.   So Jesus, the artist, went and mingled with the multitudes, "rejoiced with them that did rejoice and wept with them that wept."   He flung himself with a divine fury against a mountain of materialism, bruised and battered by the resisting stone but never losing the artist's faith that He, the image of God, was in the mountain of the multitude.   This mountain multitude was made up of living blocks.   And Jesus, after He had the vision of the perfect image of Himself in humanity, addressed Himself not to the multitude but to the individual person, the way of entrance into the whole human race.   He created the image in the separate block.   He preached to the woman of Samaria, to Nicodemus, and to any one person who crossed His path.   And He brought all the truth and power of God to bear upon that one image.   He dealt with truth concretely.

He spoke of faith and found it in the man by His side.   He found prayer and built on it in the woman at His feet. He pointed to the Kingdom of Heaven in the little child. He left the multitude for the man, as the only way to help the multitude. He was apparently indifferent to the crowd, knowing full well the emptiness of words in themselves and appreciating that soil has to be prepared before you can make things grow. So He preached to the crowd in parables that seeing they might not see, and hearing they might not understand, saying to the mountain, "Wait until I have created the image in the separate stone."

Jesus took a few men out of the mass and preached to them as an artist must preach. He taught them by making them teachers. He helped them by making them helpers. He gave to them by making them givers. He forgave them by making them forgivers. And the image within the man grew, breaking through the resisting, encrusting material, out into the Vision. And the image knew itself the image of its God, possessing in itself a creative instinct and a redeeming impulse and became endued with the power to become a preacher, who in his turn throws himself with passion upon some new resisting material to create the image there. "Until we all come unto a perfect man, unto the measure of the stature of the fulness of Christ and the image of God."

## II

### THE ARTIST'S TOOLS

WE have seen in the previous lecture that the preacher's work is so to mold the divine image within the nature of man that it will know itself alive and see. In order to do that the preacher must come in vital touch with humanity—men moving. He must act upon his knowledge that humanity is made up of individuals, and he must see with the artist's eye, through every darkness and disappointment, this divine image in every man. In order to see it in the other man, it must be alive and seeing in himself, with power to transmit its spirit into the other man, touching the sleeping spirit and awakening it to life.

Thus far, it might be said that we have described what ought properly to go on in the relation of man to man. Every man ought to influence every other man. That is true. But I have called attention to it specifically as the preacher's preparation for his preaching. The art of preaching is to transmit spirit and influence spirit by means of *words*. But before he uses words the preacher must prepare himself for their use. The artist is an artist not only when he sits down before his canvas and takes his brush in hand, or before his marble to cut the rebellious stone. He is an artist all the time; dif-

42478

ferent from other men every moment of his life.
Every time that the artist looks at a tree or a sunset
or a rock, he sees with an artist's eye, and it is preparation for the moment when his hand takes up the
tool.  You are not going to become a preacher
when you begin to write your sermon or stand in
the pulpit; you are a preacher every moment of the
time that you are jostled by the crowd, or look into
the face of men.  Your attitude toward the multitude and the individual is different from the attitude of other men, because you are to use your experience in a different way.

But as an artist you cannot yet take up your tools,
for if preaching is the art of transmitting spirit,
of influencing and molding spirit by means of words,
the preacher must know as much as he can of the
spiritual world which he is to describe in words.
And so the preacher must be able to express and
describe in words that spirit of which man's nature
is an image; he must know the spiritual world—
its geography, its constitution, its laws, principles,
and its inhabitants.  This spiritual world is not
some place where men may sometime go; it is a
world where all men live.  The work of the artist
preacher is not to prove the existence of such a
world, before man's acceptance of it, to get men to
emigrate thither; it is to open men's eyes to see
where they are already living.

The preacher finds himself in possession of doctrines and dogmas and creeds; the nature of this
spiritual world has been revealed.  The revelation
can be found in a book.  The book tells of the rela-

tionship of God, the creator, and Christ, the revealer
and savior, and the operation of the Holy Spirit
which proceeds out of that relationship. Now,
what is the preacher going to do? Is he going to
deliver the substance of this revelation in so many
words, and address it to the other man's under-
standing, trusting, if the man understands and ac-
cepts the doctrine intellectually, that it will affect
the image hidden within and open the eyes of the
man's soul, saying to himself "what a man thinks
that he is," and thinking to himself that that means
he is intellectual? The preacher, if he is an artist
with any realization of his responsibility, if he has
any vision of the image hidden in the other man,
if he is conscious of the image of God in himself, will do nothing of the kind. That is beginning at the wrong end. It is true, everlastingly
true, that "what a man thinks that he is." Doctrines and creeds are essential to living, but begin
with a doctrine and you begin at the wrong end.
"What a man thinks that he is," is true, because
of the prior truth that what a man is, that he thinks.

These doctrines that a preacher finds in his possession, what are they but the declarations of what
men have found in life in the spiritual world. They
have grown out of living. Doctrines and creeds
are the signals flying over the spiritual world, telling a man what he is to find there for himself, and
he cannot enter into the meaning of the signal, or
doctrine, until he himself has gone down deep into
spiritual experience and found what the signal has
told him he would find. Man is ever sensitive to

spiritual impressions. Out of experience he collects spiritual facts, through a faculty of his nature which we call faith. All the time his mind is registering and classifying these spiritual facts or truths and forming them into a doctrine. Every man has a doctrine of this kind, his mind's recognition and classification of those impressions.

What I am trying to say is that seeing spiritual things comes first and does not grow out of doctrine but doctrine out of seeing. You have to see before you can speak. Therefore, the artist preacher cannot be content with taking doctrines, no matter how true they are, approaching and appealing to the mind of the other man. That kind of speaking will never pass on from the mind to affect the hidden image within. All that is easy but ineffective and has gone under the name of preaching for many generations. Do you, then, not believe in intellectual preaching? Certainly I do. In more intellect than most of us have. But intellectual preaching does not consist in learning and putting forth a set of doctrines with intent to gain the assent of another mind. Intellectual preaching is the expression of a trained mind that has examined actual spiritual experiences in his own nature and in the nature of others, classifying them, coordinating them and valuing them. And so, as I have said before, if preaching is to be a fine art, if it is to make the image hidden within see, the artist must be a master of the laws and principles of the spiritual world, experienced in his own life. And that calls for the keenest mind, fastened upon the deepest living, with the utmost consecration.

It is very hard to be an artist. The revelation of God and the laws and principles of the spiritual life, how did they come to man? Were they written across the heavens? No. Were they first written in a book? No. Were they addressed in logical terms to the human mind? No. They were written in the blood of human experience, culminating in the blood of the Son of Man, and afterwards translated into words in books, and in *The Book*. And the artist, before ever he takes up his tools, has to translate those words that are in books back into human experience, back into his own experience. "Man is made in the image of God." That is the artist's starting point. It states the case in so many words. What is the artist going to do with it? Is he to pass those words on to some other man? Not if he is an artist. These words are on a sign post, pointing down into the deep world of the spirit, telling what human experience has found there and pointing the way. He, the artist, is made in the image of God. Well then, of what nature is the God in whose image he is?

Now I am not writing a treatise on theology. I am pointing out what the artist has to do, and I merely take an illustration true of his whole method. This God, in whose image the artist is, so loved the world that He gave His only begotten son, that whosoever believeth in Him should not perish but have everlasting life. "This God," says the guide post, "loves." Then the God-image within the artist loves. But it is not sufficient for the artist simply to be told that the God-image hidden within him loves. To find out what love is, he must love as God loves. He does not receive the truth just by knowing with his mind that God loves him, or that somebody else loves him. He must have the love that God has, a suffering love, a giving and a forgiving love. God is merciful. It is not sufficient for the artist to know that God is merciful to him. He must possess the quality of mercy that pertains to God. Now where is he to find that mercy which is in the nature of God? You answer, and you answer rightly, in the revelation of the life of His Son, Jesus Christ. But we are still dealing with a word. The artist has still to find the thing itself, the mercy of the Christ in the lives of human beings. It calls him out of his closet and from his books, back to moving humanity and to the individual within this moving humanity, to experience the mercy that is in the nature of God, revealed in Jesus Christ. "The blood of Jesus Christ cleanses men from sin." That is a profound truth lying at the heart of life, but the artist does not proceed to take that truth and try to satisfy the mind of the other man as to its reasonableness and effectiveness. His is a much more laborious process than that. That statement is to him a finger, pointing down into the depths of divine human life where he must go and experience for himself the operation of the universal law—how the shedding of blood for others can cleanse his own soul.

This guide post with its pointing finger has stood on the edge of the world for nineteen hundred years, and men had come to look at it, not as a guide post, but as an altar with an inscription to which they could give an intellectual assent which would in some mysterious way cleanse them from their sins. Many repudiated it, until suddenly the earth was moved and the sun darkened, and a whole generation was taken down deep into the grim and revealing realities of life. In the great war men found that what they had considered a mere intellectual statement was a universal law of life—the relation of the shedding of blood to the cleansing of the soul, and they found the Christ of the cross dying and living in the center of the world.

In speaking of the artist preacher's own preparation for his preaching, I have gone far enough, I trust, to have you men realize that the possession of these doctrines, mastered and buttressed by your learning, is but the beginning of your preparation. Each of them has to be illuminated by your own personal experience. You must have something vital in you that corresponds and answers to the description that you give of God and the spiritual life. It may be but the flickering of a candle which lights the truth dimly, but you must see something of the truth in your own nature before you dare to utter the truth. Your image must see as God sees. You must know yourself a creator, a redeemer, and then you will find yourself possessed of a power which proceeds out of that relationship to sanctify the life of your fellow men. I am aware of the fact that this statement can be twisted and misunderstood. I know perfectly well that man is not God, but I know that man can enter into God's creation not alone by being created but by creating! that man can enter into Christ's redemption not alone by being redeemed, but by redeeming! that man can enter into the sanctification by the Holy Spirit, not alone by being sanctified but by sanctifying.

I have not tried to show you what you will find by this process. I have simply indicated the process by means of which the artist prepares himself for his preaching. If the artist is so preparing himself, he will, of course, find that the Bible is his handbook. Just as the artist sculptor goes to Greece, so does the artist preacher go to Palestine. The spiritual soil of Greece produced in marble the thing of beauty that is a joy forever. The spiritual soil of Palestine produced in human nature the perfect image of God that is a joy for evermore. Therefore, the sculptor studies the land of Greece. He goes there for his models. The actual soil holds little interest. If he spends his time learning the geography and history, he is an antiquarian, not an artist. If he learns the language, he does it not as an end but as a means by which he enters into the spirit which is Greece. His one question is, How did these people create the things they did? What is the nature of the soil that made these things grow?

In the same way the artist preacher goes to Palestine, which is the Bible, or to the Bible which is Palestine. He may know the geography of Palestine, the names of every mountain and town and river, and not know anything of the real Bible. He

may know by heart all the Kings of Israel and all
the wars, and still not know anything of the Bible.
If he learns the Hebrew language, as every preacher
ought to learn it, it is not as an end but a means by
which he may catch some of the spirit which is the
Hebrew.   The Bible is an exhibit showing how
the spirit working on another spirit calls forth the
divine image.   It is just so many words hot from
the blood of a people, and these words have to be
translated back again into blood.   The Hebrews
started in a dim way with this fundamental truth,
that God made man in His own image.   They may
have had a poor idea of God and an inadequate
conception of His image.   They may not at first
have been conscious of the full truth, but they were
groping in the right direction and their history is a
description of how men through the experiences of
life were shown how to find the hidden image.
They blundered, they stumbled; but they stumbled
up instead of down.   They lost sight of the true
image and set up false ones, but prophetic voices
from within called them back to their quest.   And
they went on building up their own spiritual nature
and discovering a spiritual nature in the other man.
"Hark the dominant persistence, till it must be answered to.   Then the octave struck the answer," and
the answer was Christ, the Jesus of Bethlehem and
Nazareth and Capernaum and Jerusalem.   The
Christ, the express image of God.   A large part
of the Old Testament is a record of mistakes, of
how not to find the hidden image.   But it is invaluable because it is a description of mistakes in the

right direction. The New Testament is a description of the revelation of the true image, and also of how the consummate artist worked on the hidden image of the other man to make it see. And so to the artist preacher the Bible is indispensable and invaluable, and in fact, his all in all. But it is nothing to him but words until he translates these words into life, in terms of experience. I am speaking too generally and I am afraid I shall not be understood. What I am saying may be a truism. I do not care whether it is or not. It is in any case all important.

The Bible is a revelation of God's image, and this revelation was given to men through their daily experiences,—fighting, hating, loving, killing, blessing, eating, drinking, buying, selling, living, dying. And this revelation was put into words, preserved in words. But man does not receive the revelation that the words preserve until he enters into the experience by which the revelation came. "Blessed are the peace-makers" is a truth preserved in words. It is a revelation from God. You do not receive the revelation until you yourself are a peace-maker. In other words, you do not obtain a revelation and then proceed to be something; you are something, and by so being you receive the revelation. The preacher who does not have a definition of peace made out of his own experiences ought not to preach peace. He has not received the revelation from God that entitles him to preach, although he may have the Bible in his hand with his finger on the chapter and the verse.

In my boyhood, we used to have maps of the dif-

ferent parts of the world, bound in what we called
an atlas. We studied it on Monday through Friday
with a vacation on Saturday. And on Sunday we
had an atlas of Palestine, to our minds entirely different and unrelated. A place, if it was a place at
all, situated somewhere between earth and heaven.
And now General Allenby has ridden triumphantly
through Bethlehem and Jerusalem and has placed
Palestine on the map of the world. In the same
manner, the truths that grew out of the soil of Palestine, looked upon as something separate and apart,
unrelated to the truths growing out of other soils,
have been found to be the revelation of the laws
and principles running through all life. The In-
carnation and the Atonement have been placed on
the map of the world. The Bible is a description
of what is going on now! We have been speaking
of the preparation of the preacher for his preaching, of the necessity of the preacher artist's having
an unconquerable conviction that the divine image
is in every man, and also the necessity of the artist's
having a realization of the image in himself, expe-
riencing in himself the character of God in whose
image he is, and possessing a handbook which when
translated into experience can show him how spirit
can communicate itself to spirit, to make the hidden
image see.

An artist, so prepared, is ready to take up his
tools and go to work. A preacher is to convey,
*by means of words,* his spirit to the spirits of other
men to make the image hidden within them see—
*by means of words.* Every preacher before he

begins to write his first sermon ought to have a thorough course in Browning's, "The Ring and the Book," to learn the value of words. And before every sermon the artist preacher should read the conclusion:

"So, British public, this lesson,
  That our human speech is naught,
  Our human testimony false, our fame
  And human estimation, words and wind.
  Why take the artistic way to prove so much?
  Because it is the glory and good of art,
  That art remains the one way possible
  Of speaking truth, to mouths like mine, at least.
  How look a brother in the face and say
  Thy right is wrong, eyes hast thou, yet art blind.
  Thine ears are stuffed and stopped, despite their
      length,
  And oh, the foolishness, thou countest faith.
  Say this as silvery as tongue can troll—
  The anger of the man may be endured.
  The shrug, the disappointed eyes of him
  Are not so bad to bear—but here's the plague
  That all this trouble comes of telling truth,
  Which truth, by when it reaches him looks false,
  Seems to be just the thing it would supplant,
  Nor recognizable by whom it left
  While falsehood would have done the work of
      truth
  But art—wherein man nowise speaks to men
  Only to mankind—art may tell a truth
  Obliquely, do the thing shall breed the thought
  Nor wrong the thought, missing the mediate word
  So may you paint your picture, twice show truth

Beyond mere imagery on the wall—
So, note by note, bring music from your mind,
Deeper than e'en Beethoven divined,
So write a book shall mean beyond the facts
Suffice the eye and save the soul beside."

And this brings us around the circle to what we said at the beginning. The sermon is but a tool and should be approached and worked upon as a tool. The art of the preacher does not consist in making sentences or literature, or constructing a sermon according to a perfect model. His art consists in so using his sermon that it will convey spirit to the spirit of the other man, to make his hidden image see. The artist has the image of God and not the sermon tool in mind. Now, what I am going to say, I beg of you not to take too literally. I am depending on the fact that you possess imagination. If you have not imagination you can never be a good preacher. I am going to describe a process. My description and explanation of the process may be in many respects wrong, but the process I know to be right. A wireless station in this country conveys a message to Paris. I may not be accurate in my explanation of how it is done, but that it is done there can be no doubt. You are starting to write a sermon, and I emphasize *write,* because every preacher ought to *write* one sermon a week for certainly ten years. You have become aware of the pathetic, tragic, moving multitude; you have had one instance of human blindness brought home to you, and you have brought it home into your workshop. You have within yourself a real-

ization of the image of God. And you see it in
the other man and want to make his hidden image
come forth. Out of a Book you take words which
have sprung out of the blood of human experience,
revealing the healing properties and regenerating
principles that are in the heart of God, and you
translate them back into your own experience, and
the spiritual meaning is revealed to you. After
that, you have to translate that spirit back again
into your own words, dipped in blood, that have a
special bearing upon the immediate case before you,
so that *with every word you utter* there goes the
corresponding spirit. With every word you utter
there goes the corresponding spirit. Your princi-
pal attention is fastened upon the *image* hid within
the other man. Your chief object is to make it see.

Before you do that, you have to use your tool,
your sermon, in such a manner that you catch the
man's attention and arouse his interest and awaken
his mind. It may be by the skill of your sentences,
or your apt illustrations. You have to deal with
a certain amount of resisting and recalcitrant stone.
And that is where the right construction of your
tool comes in. Work on your tool until it does perfect work, but beware lest you spend your time on
unnecessary adornment. See that the tool cuts the
stone, but do not spend valuable time on the polishing of the handle, for all this is preliminary and sub-
sidiary. Your tool is to cut away the surrounding
and resisting material, but it is also to fashion the
image, or awaken the image so that it may see. And
that is where the spirit that accompanies the words

does its work. The spirit sometimes goes with the word, sometimes ahead of it; it touches hidden springs in unexpected ways, it receives our orders and disobeys them, it obeys laws which we do not yet understand and coöperates with forces that are far beyond us, it forges its own invisible tools and works on the image in imperceptible ways, and the image is built to music and therefore never built, and therefore built forever.

If you will put the spirit into the word, the word, as Browning says, may mean to the man just the opposite from what it meant to you; but the spirit interprets it and works in its own way. You will be surprised to find in a real sermon how little the words count. They are absolutely necessary and they must be the right words in the right place and mean something. But the real art of the preacher is to tip the point of the word with spirit and let that spirit fashion in its own way the man and make him see. It may not reach the image of the man in your workshop, you may never know whom it does reach and fashion, but you *can* know this— that if the word is tipped with spirit in the way we have described, that spirit is bound to form the power to see in some image of God. Any blindness in any man is the entrance into the universal nature of man, through which the word tipped with spirit can enter to make blind eyes see. Write your sermon, direct your tool to the man in your workshop, see that your work is tipped with spirit, and leave the rest to God. You will never see the result of your artistry, as the sculptor sees the image he has hewn out of the stone, but it exists somewhere, if you have tipped your word with fire.

The operation of spiritual laws is inevitable and inexorable. Given a word freighted with the spirit, that word will go to its destination, and the spirit will surely touch the blinded soul and the blinded soul will surely see.

We have seen in what way the artist must put his spirit into the word. And now we come to the method of Jesus, the consummate artist, in working upon His material, which method we touched upon at the close of our first lecture. This is most important, and if you will get hold of the idea it will affect your preaching all the days of your life. Here is a man, let us say, John, in Jesus' workshop, with the image of God hidden within him. Jesus was to take that son of thunder and make him know himself the Son of God. He was to change the spirit of adventure into an adventure of the spirit, so that John might see. Now John was a frail mortal and needed help; he was ignorant and needed knowledge; a sinner, he needed forgiveness, and Jesus stood in His workshop between the image hidden within the nature of John and the infinite inexhaustible resources stored up in the living God. Jesus stood between the Giver and the prospective recipient of the gift, with the gift in His hand. I ask you to picture John *facing* Jesus with hands outstretched to receive the gift of the spirit of the image, and then I ask you to have this act of Jesus burned forever on your mind. Jesus took John, who was facing Him to receive the gift, and turned

him around, turned him around completely, making
him face in the direction that Jesus faced, and so
making John receive the gift in the only way that
it could be received,—by making John a giver.
That is one of the critical moments in the history
of the world, when John was *turned around*—when
he no longer faced Jesus with his hands stretched
out to receive, but walked *with* Jesus with his hands
stretched out to his fellows to give.   And I beg
you to notice this, that John did not turn around
because he saw, but Jesus turned him around in
order to make him see.

This is so fundamental and important that we
must dwell upon it.   If you give a man a book,
that book is an expression of your giving nature.
The man facing you has received a thing, a book,
but he has not received your giving nature which
is God's nature, until he turns around, and walks
with you and gives himself, and then, and only
then, he receives and knows in that giving aspect your image and the image of God.   You, a
teacher, give a man a truth.   He has not received
it until he himself becomes a teacher and can express and give that truth, which is God's truth.
You, a preacher, tell a man that needs mercy that
God is merciful.   You have not given that man
anything.   He has not received anything until you,
an artist, have in some way turned that man
around and made him a merciful man, and then, and
only then, has he received the quality of mercy
which is an aspect of the image of God.   A man
does not receive mercy and then go forth to give it.

He does not receive it until he gives it. A man comes to a preacher and faces him, asking for God's forgiveness, and the preacher cannot give him forgiveness until, becoming an artist, he turns him around and makes that man a forgiver, and then, and only then, does that man's image know itself to be made in the image of a forgiving God.

A man in sorrow stands before a preacher crying out for comfort, and the artist puts God's comfort into the man's nature by making him a comforter. That was the method of the fine art of Jesus. He chose a man out of the multitude and took him into His workshop, taught him God's truth by making him a teacher of God's truth. And the man taught and saw. He brought God's help to man by making the man a helper and the man helped and the image of God within him saw still more. He brought the forgiveness of God to a man suffering for his sins by making a man suffer in forgiving other men's sins. And the man suffered and the image of God within him could see still more. And the man was tested by fire and came out of the crucible, a creator, a redeemer and a comforter of men, seeing the invisible world of the spirit in which he lived.

It is all summed up in this principle of Jesus. He made the individual give help to the multitude not primarily for the sake of the multitude but for the sake of the individual.

If a preacher becomes an artist and follows the method of Jesus, his sermons take on a different character. If he is preaching to the sorrowful, he does not say words of comfort (that is comparatively easy). He creates an atmosphere which calls for and produces pity and mercy in the sorrowful soul, and lo, the sorrow disappears. But I can not stop to pursue this thought. I only say that the character of the sermon changes the moment the preacher becomes the artist and follows the method of Jesus, when he thinks of men, not as facing him but as walking with him. Whenever you are about to begin a sermon and you have in mind some pathetic face out of the multitude looking up appealingly into your face, do not begin your sermon until you have *turned* that *man around,* and think of him as going with you, and I promise you that the character of your sermon will be very different. If you talk to John when he is facing you, you are trying to make him see through the back of his head. But if you will turn John around, your conversation will be spared many unnecessary arguments, for he will see what you are seeing, and what is more, he will see with his own eyes.

In treating preaching as a fine art, you may say that I have dwelt upon the artist preacher in the marketplace, jostled and hurt by the moving multitude, and in his closet with his God, and in his study with his book, and with his man with the image hidden within him, and that I have seemed oblivious of the fact that there was such a thing as a pulpit where a preacher is supposed to stand and preach to a number of people called a congregation sitting in the pews.

No, I have not forgotten. It has been in my

mind through everything I have said. The pulpit is the preacher's throne, which he may ascend only as he shows his royal blood and the right of succession. If his credentials are merely a literary masterpiece, wrought with perfect art in his fully equipped library, to be delivered with the silver tongue of an orator, he cannot enter there. But if he stands at the steps of the pulpit in the spirit of an artist, with a vision that comes with the realization of the image of God within him, and a consuming and over-mastering passion to bring out that image in the other man; if he comes sweating, as it were, drops of blood from the dashing of himself against a hard, cruel, cold humanity, with the unconquerable faith that never forgets the image within the stone; if he has heard some particular cry and has wrestled with an individual man to turn him around and make him see, then the doors of the pulpit are thrown open to him and he ascends his throne with power, a throne that no other artist dare ascend, for the materials are living souls, and the tools are words tipped with spirit, and the purpose is participation in the creation of the image of God.

There is nothing equal to its terrible responsibility. Before him are invisible images in all stages of development, waiting for the authoritative touch. About him are unseen armies of creative spirits, waiting for the authoritative command; walls and roofs disappear, and earth and sky are rolled up like a scroll, and the preacher stands with these images of God before him in a spiritual world, based on eternal principles and governed by eternal law. What shall issue from the preacher out of the eternal silence? That which came forth at the beginning, a word, but a word made flesh and living among us, a word that has agonized and bled and died and come to life again, a word born of the spirit. And the word with the wings of the spirit flies with an unerring instinct to the image that is crying for its touch. And because of the preacher's word, the man sees, not perhaps the one the artist has worked upon, not in the way he would have chosen, but inevitably, surely, the spirit finds its way. You shoot an arrow into the air; it falls to earth you know not where. So will that word of the spirit find and do its work in some son of God.

If a preacher really seizes hold of a spiritual principle, he need not go afield for his symbols and illustrations, for with every spiritual principle the inevitable symbol waits close at hand. If you do not find the symbol waiting for you, it is a sign that you have not grasped the principle. Here, for instance, is the law of the hungry soul and the truth of the life that feeds it. And here, not far afield, but close to it, bound in it, is the inevitable symbol of the bread and wine.

Any word that the preacher may utter, born in spirit and in blood, will find its inevitable symbol, and it will also be related to all other words with their separate content, and will link itself with the universal scheme of things, the law and principles of creation and redemption and judgment.

Any one who stands in the Sistine Chapel in Rome will see above him Michael Angelo's idea of the creation, God, the artist, with beings in the folds of His garment, representing relationship and abundant life, stretching out his hand and touching the image of man to create it in the image of God. And at the eastern end of the Chapel is the great picture of the Day of Judgment with men made in the image of God falling and rising, and all around the walls is the story of the life of Christ, from the cradle to the Cross, and from the Cross to the Ascension. But it is all together, bound together in the one and the same room. And if you stop before the cradle to tell about that, behind it is the creation and beside it the crucifixion, before it is the Judgment. The whole sweep of God's purposes and plans is poured into the picture of the cradle. Any word that you as an artist utter (if it is worth anything at all, and if it is not, then God have mercy on your soul), any word you preach that is worth anything at all has behind it God's eternal creation, and within it the Cross, and before it the Judgment of a living, loving God.

The tale is as old as the Eden Tree, as
   New as the new cut tooth,
For each man knows e'er his lip thatch grows,
   He is master of wit and truth.
And each man hears as the twilight nears
   To the beat of the dying heart
The Devil drum on the darkened pane.  You
   Did it, but was it art?

We have learned to whittle the Eden
    Tree to the shape of a surplice-peg.
We have learned to bottle our parents twain
    In the yoke of an addled egg.
We know that the tail must wag the dog,
    As the horse is drawn by the cart
But the devil whoops as he whoops of old
    It's clever, but is it art?

No, it is not art. And that is why so much
preaching is a woful, sinful failure. You are a master of art. Quit from this moment being satisfied
with the polishing of your tool. See the need and
hear the cry of a suffering humanity, as expressed
in the individual. Find the answer in terms of life,
as expressed in Jesus Christ. Suffer as an artist
must suffer. Agonize. Shed your blood, and the
spirit of the Eternal God will pour through you to
touch the spirit of the other man; and it will be given
you what to say; and you will speak with the tongue
of angels. Each one of you here can be a great
preacher, if each in your separate star you will form
in some other life the image of God as *you* see it
and feel it and know it, for the God of things as
they are.

That's art. Amen. So be it.